THE GOETIA HYMNS

REV. CAIN

Copyright © 2021 by Rev. Cain

All rights reserved.

This is a work of religious nature, and the information herein is intended solely for educational purposes.

You are responsible for yourself, your actions, and how you conduct yourself as a human being – not us, and not anyone else.

Act responsibly, and conduct yourself in a way that exemplifies honor, integrity, and decency towards yourself and those around you.

AUTHOR'S PREFACE

It has been my life's calling, to artfully study and explore the Left-Hand Path with the hope of easing the drought of knowledge that afflicts *both* theistic Satanism and the ancient art of demonology – and, in this endeavor, I have exceeded my expectations.

I say this not with arrogance, but with *elation* – the occult is a wild beast, and to attempt to bring some degree of order to it is a madman's pursuit – even madder when the beast bears the name of Satanism or demonic magic – inherently *untamable* colossi.

It is, then, perhaps more accurate to say that I have *redirected* these beasts towards a path that is truer to their nature – entwined as one, and born from a chapter of our history that has had its soul bled dry.

In my every manuscript, I strive to write with both power and poeticism – to rekindle the dying flame of strength within the heart of devilry, while *also* providing beauty, art, and spirituality to the reader.

Until now, no more evident was this in my writing than with our demonological grimoires – lauded in over 100 countries around the world for the power, knowledge, and inspiration they offer to occultists.

These grimoires are staples in *thousands* of occult libraries, and the general belief is that these books are some of the most effective demonological texts in existence, for they achieve what few others *ever* attempt – the successful harmonization of wisdom, history, poeticism, and unholy, liturgical scripture.

With *The Goetia Hymns*, I endeavored to author a manuscript that bore the qualities of our grimoires, yet offered something unique and *refreshing* to the occultists of the Left-Hand Path – a compendium of theistic, liturgical hymns and prayers, penned in honor of the 72 devils of the *Ars Goetia* hierarchy.

As I express throughout our myriad books, the art of demonology is a cornerstone of theistic Satanic worship – one *cannot* adhere to the Left-Hand Path of theistic Satanism while excluding demonology from their studies – they must coexist, or you must find an atheistic iteration of Satanism to follow.

If you are to follow a path of theistic Satanism, you *must* understand that knowledge itself is only *one* part of the equation – this faith demands prayer, as well as the emotional investment of the disciple in Satan, our kingdom of Hell, and the devils therein.

It is my hope that, through *The Goetia Hymns*, you are able to kindle a closer relationship with Hell's most prominent devils – that you shall feel a sense of sanctuary, strength, and kinship as you hail their thrones in search of empowerments and blessings.

On the Left-Hand Path of theistic Satanism, devils will be your greatest allies – they are your gateway to our kingdom of Hell, prepared at all times to aid those that proudly bear the burning mark of Satan.

I thank you for taking the time to read this – may your Left-Hand Path be wrought with all fruits and pleasures that your bestial heart desires – and may *The Goetia Devils* aid you in their acquisition.

– Rev. Cain
Salem, MA

TO THE REVERED DEVILS OF PERDITION.

BY THE UNHALLOWED GRACE OF SATAN,

ILLUMINATED AND GLORIOUS SHEPHERED OF FIRE.

REVEREND CAIN WISHES GLORY, HEREIN, UNTO THE BLACKENED FIELDS OF HELL.

Endless were the fruits of Satan, our Infernal Lord in fire – the unholy bounties bestowed upon us, the horned children – the unrepentant apostles of Hell!

When first he descended before us, upon a chariot of cindered ash, enlightenment befell us – and our souls found power through the light of darkness.

In Satan's reviled name, I honor the path that waits ahead, paved with sulfur and fire – lead me to your nectarous groves and the eternal kingdom of Hell!

THE INFERNAL DEDICATORY

As Satan touches our souls with fire, we will know of his salvation – he will shepherd us, and guide us through the despondent twilight of eternity.

And with his sulfuric touch, we may feel the divine ichor of devils permeate our hearts – and our atria will flood with the vigor of Satan's throne.

Through his deliverance, we shall know him as the sovereign light, and savior – our crusader sheathed in the glorious fires of the kingdom of Hell.

THE NAMES AND ORDER OF ALL THE HYMNS & PRAYERS OF HELL

AUTHOR'S PREFACE	5
THE INFERNAL DEDICATORY	11
INTRODUCTION	27
STRENGTH, COURAGE & POWER	31
THE EBON PATH	33
SAINT OF SANCTUARY	34
AEGIRUS FIERUM	35
ON WINGS OF SULFUR	36
IN HELLFIRE	37
O' CERBERUS	38
POPHECCIUS	39
ODE TO BEASTS	40

CIVIPALLAS	41
PROTECTION & WARDING	43
MIVORUS SANCTUM	45
IN SATAN'S SHADOW	46
AN IVORY FLAME	47
TERRICASSO	48
O' RONOVE	49
ECLIPSE OF FORNEUS	50
SANCTUS ETUM STYX	51
ODE TO ABRAXAS	52
O' MARCHOSIAS	53
THE VIPER'S BANE	54
NOCTESSIX	55
ODE TO CIMERIES	56
OPHIDEUX II	57
OF THESE HALLS	58
THE APOSTLE'S SCAR	59

O' ZAGAN 60

THE FORTRESS SOUL 61

CARAPACE 62

HEALTH, LIFE & WELLBEING 63

TRANQUILLO 65

THE LIGHT OF BUER 66

THE SPAN OF DEVILS 67

PLAGEUS ROVEMA 68

HYMN OF HEALING 69

ODE TO SABNOCK 70

SINEUS ETUM HETHES 71

A FEARLESS FIRE 72

ODE TO PESTILENCE 73

MIRE OF FEAR 74

DISCOVERY & REVELATIONS 75

VASSAGO'S VEIL 77

ATULLA PREMOSO 78

THE ROAD BEHIND	79
O' ANDROMALIUS	80
VURTUM SECRIMO	81
THE ROAD AHEAD	82
ODE TO AAMON	83
QUISIMO MOLDES	84
TORCH OF CIMERIES	85
EXPELLA OCCULO	86
NIGHT OF VUAL	87
WITHIN HER DEPTHS	88
IN DARKLING FAITH	89
O' PAIMON	90
PRETAMA REVELLES	91
THE EYES OF VINE	92
ADVERSARY OR ALLY	93
KNOWLEDGE & ILLUMINATION	95
ODE TO IPOS	97

AMPLIFASSO	98
OF SAGES & DEVILS	99
THE PALL OF MALPHAS	100
ILLYRIA MALLIOS	101
MY BURNING WORD	102
ODE TO MARBAS	103
HYMNESSIAS	104
ON HERMETIC WINDS	105
ARTEMOS IMPRESSA	106
ODE TO APOSTLES	107
DIABOSA ETHES SACRUM	108
THE LIGHT OF BARBATOS	109
O' ASTAROTH	110
ODE TO PUCEL	111
VIVISSIO DAEMAS	112
THE HORNED APOSTLE	113
THE BLACK ARTS	115

FROM HEAVEN'S HULL.................... 117
HERMETAS INGLOMIO..................... 118
THE VOID – SHE WHISPERS............. 119
IN WINTER'S NAME 120
AN EMBERLESS PATH 121
COSMECCIA 122
OF EARTH & ETHER........................... 123
ODE TO ORIAS 124
LUNASERE APPIRUM........................ 125
THE LIGHTLESS CRAFT.................... 126
IN SOOT & SHADOW 127
HAUTEM ETUUS DI'ABO................... 128
ODE TO ALLOCES............................... 129
FROM THE FIRES 130
OF BLOOD & DARKNESS.................. 131
METAPHYSICALITY 133
SHEPHERD OF SOULS 135

ADELPHIA VISUCCI	136
OF SOULS DEPARTED	137
THE SIGHT OF CAIM	138
INNUX ETUUS XUNNI	139
DAMNED & DEPARTED	140
PRETACCIO MEDUMASI	141
THE CHILL OF MURMUR	142
ODE TO BERITH	143
TO SEE – TO DREAM	144
OF GLORY & GRANDEUR	145
WEALTH, RICHES & SUCCESS	147
HIS GILDED FIRES	149
ODE TO ANDROMALIUS	150
THE PATH TO WEALTH	151
OCEANS OF GOLD	152
COFFICCI ALORIDA	153
OF GILDED FLAME	154

THE FRUITS OF GUSION 155
INSPIRIA VI'ELLA 156
MY WEALTH RETURNED 157
ODE TO ASMODEUS 158
LOVE, SEX & HEDONISM 159
VASSAGO'S HEARTH 161
HEDONOS APPETIVA 162
HEARTH & HELLFIRE 163
CUPIDASO PROVOCCI 164
ODE TO RAUM 165
HARMONISSO 166
ATTELLIS PI'RUUA 167
O' FORNEUS 168
GARDEN OF MARCHOSIAS 169
HYMN OF SALLOS 170
ONCE – TWICE MINE 171
SUCCUBI OF ZEPAR 172

CARNALLA ETUUS HEDOMOS	173
MALLAMIA SUCCUMOS	174
ODE TO ZAGAN	175
O' BELETH	176
TRUTH & VENGEANCE	177
THE FURY OF FURFUR	179
IN BLOOD AND MOONFALL	180
DEBALMA AXEGASO	181
THE COURT OF MINOS	182
INSALLOS MEDUMIA	183
WINTER'S BLIGHT	184
A SOUL CONDEMNED	185
GRIEVIASSO	186
EXECUMA TERRIDOS	187
ODE TO ELIGOS	188
THE FIRES OF FLAUROS	189
VINE'S TITHE	190

GENERAL WICKEDNESS 191
  OF HOWLING TEMPESTS 193
  RAUM'S RUINATION 194
  HYSPIRIA MOLLOM 195
  THE MIND'S DECAY 196
  SOUL & SINEWS 197
  DAEMOS ETUUS CARRAS 198
  THE CRUEL & THE PIOUS 199
  LOVE, UNDONE 200
  HAUTELLAS AMORTEMA 201
  THE HAUNTING OF AGARES 202
  ODE TO AIM 203
  O' FOCALOR 204
  OF SPECTERS AND ILLUSIONS 205
  AN EPOCH OF MADNESS 206
  MEDUNNAS LI'BELLOS 207
  ODE TO CHAOS 208

THE WITHERING OF BAEL	209
CONQUEST, STATUS & PRESTIGE	211
GIANT OF OLDE	213
AUTIGRA DOMINES	214
HOLLIMOS ETHES NI'TIRRA	215
ODE TO FORNEUS	216
AN EIDOLON OF POWER	217
OF GUSION'S GRACE	218
LUCIFUGE, THE ARBITER	219
OF SATAN'S CHOSEN	220
AMONGST DEVILS	221
IMEXIAS ETUUS SATANAS	222
THE NATURE OF DEVILS	223
IN MY HONOR	225
CHARICASSO DAEMAS	226
THE LOAM OF EDEN	227
OF TONGUE & VERSE	228

ODE TO ANDREALPHUS 229

HIS SILVER LYRE 230

LANGUILLA ETUUS DAEMAS 231

TO SPEAK AS SPIRITS 232

THE EYE OF AIM 233

IN VUAL'S EMBRACE 234

THE TRUMPETS OF HELL 235

DIVINE BLASPHEMY 237

DI'AMESSIA OCCULLIOS 239

AS HEAVEN SPILLS OVER 240

SECRIMOS ETHUS DAEMAS 241

OF HEAVEN PILLAGED 242

BEHIND IVORY GATES 243

HER APHOTIC SECRETS 244

ODE TO BATHIN 245

DAEMOSO ETUUS OMNISSIA 246

WHERE SATAN REIGNS 247

VAPULA'S HEARTH 248
HEIMESIO ETUUS PATRIXIA 249
CLOSING HONORS 251
OTHER PUBLICATIONS 253

INTRODUCTION

A compendium of demonological hymns, prayers, and rites of worship, *The Goetia Hymns* offers the reader a wealth of infernal wisdom and expression, the likes of which have never before been penned.

———

This book offers nearly 200 liturgical prayers that call upon the 72 devils of the *Ars Goetia* – the most infamous and illustrious hierarchy of devils known to humankind – the pinnacle of demonic brilliance.

These 72 devils are the original dissenters – amidst the Grand Revolt of angels in Heaven, these spirits fought alongside Satan against the tyranny of God, and they were sentenced to damnation beside him.

Once in Hell, Satan crowned these 72 demons with titles and thrones that reflected the authorities they held in Heaven, prior to the Grand Revolt – Satan trusted them, and he rewarded them for their noble actions – abetting his mutinous defiance of God.

As a theistic Satanist, these devils are your closest allies upon the Left-Hand Path – they will aid your quest for infernal illumination, and they shall offer their blessings to those judged unwavering in faith.

There have existed few manuscripts to *ever* speak of and explore the Goetia 72 in a liturgical fashion, with faith, foremost, in mind – *The Goetia Hymns* shall solidify its place in history by mere existence.

Despite this, *The Goetia Hymns* shall not *thrive* by merit of existence, but by the quality of the prayers and scriptures found within – they are some of the best that I have written, and many of them I wrote years ago for use in my work as a Satanic priest.

As well, many of these prayers I have turned to in moments of personal expression – in times of fear, rage, celebration, and further – they have served as an outlet for me to rejoice in my faith as a Satanist, to find strength through Hell in moments of dread, and to form kinships with the devils of the Goetia.

There is no right nor wrong way for you to utilize the prayers within *The Goetia Hymns*, though I did write them with theism in mind – to be recited with a literal belief in Hell, Satan, and his gallant devils.

These prayers were written to be used in moments of mortal need – that is how *I* have used them, and how I continue to use them to this day – as potent, *concise* displays of my faith as an apostle of Satan.

In moments of fragility, anxiety, wrath, terror, and sadness, you may turn to these prayers for strength and guidance from our kingdom of Hell – they will remind you of your nature as a disciple of Satan, capable of enduring the *worst* of this mortal Earth.

As they may illuminate your blackest hours, these prayers shall *also* stoke the fires of your diabolical Left-Hand Path, encouraging you to pursue all that you desire – love, wealth, sex, knowledge, power, sanctuary, and *all* other pleasurous fruits of Satan.

No matter your unique needs, the Goetia devils are waiting to hear from you – a worshipful apostle of Satan's godship, destined to our kingdom of Hell!

HYMNS AND PRAYERS

THAT MAY EVOKE

STRENGTH, COURAGE & POWER

Herein, you will find prayers that draw strength and power from our kingdom of Hell – its obsidian crags, colossal ramparts, and the glorious devils that dwell within its fires – unquenchable and inextinguishable.

These devils shall embolden those that bear the mark of Satan – their hearts shall howl with indomitability, and their souls shall thunder with vigor – unbroken by the trials, threats, and conflicts of this mortal coil.

THE EBON PATH

O' Ipos – hear me, great Prince of Hell!

As I walk the ebon path, may I feel the cindered

spirit of Hell within me – ever-burning,

and undaunted in the face of

life, Death, and God's

tyrannical will.

SAINT OF SANCTUARY

Hear me, Andromalius – devil of deliverance!

May I traverse this mortal Earth without fear, or suffering – shield me, o' hellbound saint of sanctuary – offer me asylum before your nighted throne, for I, _____,

am a worshipful apostle

of Satan!

AEGIRUS FIERUM

Aegirus Fierum – hear me, President Botis!

I, _____, call to your throne in search of
resilience, courage, and the power
of our kingdom of Hell – fill my spirit with
venom, or the vitriol of liberation – seize
my mortal heart, and flood
its atria with your
strength.

ON WINGS OF SULFUR

Hear these wicked words, Glasya-Labolas!

May you lift me above this chaos – hoist high my cinder-kissed soul, upon ashen wings of shadow and sulfur – inspirit me with your ire – your nature of unbreakable iron – and fill my heart with the howling fires of Hell!

IN HELLFIRE

Marquis of Hell, empower this apostle – Aamon!

Lend me your armaments – your sword of flame
and aegis of brimstone – sheath my hands
in unquenchable hellfire, so that I
may immolate the obstacles
that loom ahead.

O' CERBERUS

I call to you, Cerberus – horned colossus of Hell!

Hear me, and bless this disciple of Satan with your defiant nature – o' Cerberus, great beast of Hell, whose heads thrice howl in eternal glory – bathe my spirit with the fearless flames of your wicked throne!

POPHECCIUS

I speak now to a Marquis of Hell – Cimeries!

May I stand with courage before all that
threatens me, and all that wishes
harm against me – may this disciple of Satan
not fall victim to the tempests
or trespassers of this
lightless mortal
Earth.

Popheccius intemellos – bless me, Cimeries!

ODE TO BEASTS

By Hell's cinderlight, I beckon you – Amdusias!

I stand before you a loyal devotee of Satan's
diabolical congregation – bless me,
and inspire me with your heraldic song – that
demonic ode to awaken the infernal
beast that slumbers within my
embered heart.

CIVIPALLAS

Hear this errant prayer, Furcas – Knight of Hell!

*May I endure – the famine, the war, and the cold
desolation of life – may I weather her cruel
tempests, and conquer the shadows
that seethe within her icy depths – may I
withstand all that threatens
wickedness and peril
against me.*

Civipallas ertuus mogellas, Sir Furcas!

HYMNS AND PRAYERS
THAT MAY OFFER
PROTECTION & WARDING

Herein, you will find prayers that call for protection from the Goetia devils – those that bear the mark of Satan shall find sanctuary before their thrones, and safety within their cinder-sworn, unassailable guard.

As well, these devils may cleanse the disciple's path of all that bears wickedness – trespassers, the lambs of God, and errant spirits may be exiled – unwelcome wanderers will be purged from the paths of apostles.

MIVORUS SANCTUM

Mivorus sanctum – bless me, Prince Orobas!

I, _____, hail your throne in search of sanctuary – look upon my bestial heart and see his infernal mark – Satan, lord and shepherd of our ever-burning kingdom of Hell!

IN SATAN'S SHADOW

Hear me, Halphas – bloodied protector of Hell!

*May I traverse this Earth without impediment, or
threat to the flesh that sheaths my mortal
bones – may I walk safely in Satan's
shadow, free from the sorrow,
wickedness, and pain
of this leprous
world.*

AN IVORY FLAME

Hear this prayer, Botis – President of Hell!

There is an ivory flame within me, and it burns
in Satan's name – it protects me from the
mortal earth, and the serpents that
dwell upon its loam – I am
safe within the sable
arms of Hell.

TERRICASSO

Glasya-Labolas – protect me, President of Hell!

*I, _____, am an ardent apostle of Satan's
Kingdom of Hell – look upon my spirit,
and you shall see his cindered mark – know me
as a loyal celebrant, and protect me
as I weather the storms and howling tempests
of this wretched mortal Earth.*

Terricasso irrum premotivas, Glasya-Labolas.

O' RONOVE

I speak now to Ronove – great shepherd of Hell!

*O' Ronove, guide me through the darkness – this
quagmire of mortal gloom that grasps at
my weary heart – lead me through
the fields of blood and fire, to
the sanctuary asylum
of your throne.*

ECLIPSE OF FORNEUS

Marquis of Hell, protect this apostle – Forneus!

May you hear this prayer, and entomb my spirit
within your eclipse – the yawning shadow
of your throne, whose silhouette
stretches over Satan's
disciples like the hungering spear
of Goliath!

SANCTUS ETUM STYX

Hear this prayer of deliverance, Marquis Shax.

In Satan's name, I call to you – bless this apostle of Hell, and shroud me within your dreaded night – there, by the shores of the River Styx, where darkness is the light of devils and disciples alike.

Sanctus etum Styx.

Ave, Satanas.

ODE TO ABRAXAS

Abraxas – demon of the abyss – I call to you now!

O' Abraxas, shimmering star of Hell – I stand
beneath your twinkling breath, lit afire
like the lamplights of sin – and,
as I gaze supine to your eldritch bright, I ask
for your guiding aegis – shield me
within your everlasting night,
and protect me from
all that bears
malice.

O' MARCHOSIAS

In search of hearth, I call to you – Marchosias!

O' Marchosias, matriarch of Hell – caretaker
of apostles and devils the same – seize
my weary spirit, and sheath me
within your nurturing
embrace – my
heart is heavy, and sorrow
floods my mortal veins – take hold of this
disciple of Satan, and shepherd me
to strength again.

THE VIPER'S BANE

Protect this apostle of Hell – Marquise Sabnock!

I await your covetous shadow – entomb me
within your starry aegis, and protect
me from the horrors that slither and prowl
upon this mortal plane – the heralds of gloom
and their pious vipers – the harbingers
of sorrow, and those that loathe
the proud celebrants
of Satan.

NOCTESSIX

Hear this diabolical prayer, Marquis Andras!

Seize my sulfuric heart, and shroud me within
your lightless night – the darkness cast
by your dawnless throne, over
the devils and disciples
that bear the scar
of Satan!

Noctessix appritema ecclessios, Andras!

ODE TO CIMERIES

With this darkling ode, I call to you – Cimeries!

O' Cimeries – ancient devil, whose heart burns
with hellbound fire – whose spirit towers
boldly like a cathedral of iron – I,
_____, call to you now
in search of sanctuary
and your nighted
asylum!

OPHIDEUX II

Hear me, Agares – demoness of banishment!

I hear them hissing – my ophidian adversaries,
slithering beneath the shroud of shadows
that palls my Left-Hand Path – they
await my ruin, with forked tongues dripping in
wicked reverie – Duchess of Hell,
cleanse the road ahead, and
reveal those that lurk
in predation!

Ophideux exilleus moldaso, Agares!

OF THESE HALLS

Duke of Hell, cleanse this haunted place – Bune!

*O' spirits – visitors of these earthly halls, I
demand your departure – in the name of Satan
and by the force of Bune, you must now
abandon this place – you are not
welcome upon the path of
this fervent beast
of Hell!*

THE APOSTLE'S SCAR

With this infernal prayer, I call to you – Flauros!

*I, _____, am a celebrant of Hell – look
upon my wicked soul, and you shall find
the apostle's scar – for it burns in Satan's name,
may you protect me, and shield me
from all that threatens harm.*

O' ZAGAN

By Hell's sanguine light, I beckon you – Zagan!

O' Zagan, King of Hell – bless this disciple
of Satan's congregation – know me
as a shepherd of darkness, and protect me
from all that bears malice – bless me,
glorious keeper of Satan's
cindered apostles!

THE FORTRESS SOUL

Hear this prayer, King Vine – and inspire me!

In Satan's name, bless this cinder-sworn disciple of Hell – set afire my mortal spirit, and reforge it in your indomitable image – an infernal fortress, whose rampart walls shall tower beyond reach of the perils that plague this Earth.

Ave, Satanas.

CARAPACE

O' primeval demon, hearten my soul – King Bael!

Bael – infamous imperator of Hell – I call
upon you now in search of resilience – hear
this diabolical prayer, and bless me
with your spirit – bestow upon
me a carapace of brimstone and iron, so
that I may weather the sorrows
and trials that this world
may bear.

HYMNS AND PRAYERS
THAT MAY BRING
HEALTH, LIFE & WELLBEING

Herein, you will find prayers that seek health and the betterment of mind, flesh, and spirit from the devils of our kingdom of Hell – the furthering of wellbeing, and the pursuit of a long-lasting life upon this Earth.

These devils may mend the health of those that swear fealty to Satan's reign – their flesh shall strengthen, their mind shall know clarity, and their soul shall not fall prey to the tempests of our sorrowful world.

TRANQUILLO

By soothing hellfire, I hail you – Prince Orobas!

Bless me, tranquil devil – fill me with your ichor
    of unhallowed calm, and purge all anxieties
        from my grieving mind – bring peace
            to this apostle of Satan!

Tranquillo peccessi basillia – bless me, Orobas.

THE LIGHT OF BUER

Buer, President of Hell – heal this disciple!

*O' Buer, devil of replenishing grace – hear
me, and bathe me within the light
of your illustrious throne – seize my mortal
clay, and cleanse from it all
that putrefies my mind, flesh, and spirit.*

THE SPAN OF DEVILS

I call to you, Foras – revered President of Hell!

O' Foras, bearer of undying breath – hear
this wicked prayer, and bestow upon
me the span of devils – may I
thrive upon this mortal
Earth beyond my
fated years!

PLAGEUS ROVEMA

Plageus rovema – heal me, President Marbas!

I, _____, call upon your throne in search of
rejuvenation – heal the wounds that mar
my battered flesh – the sickness
that courses throughout
my veins, and threatens my mortal
life as prey – in Satan's diabolical name,
may it be so.

Ave, Satanas.

HYMN OF HEALING

O' Leraje – bless me with your healing hellfire!

*Empower this apostle of Satan – inspirit me
with your wicked grace, and teach me to soothe
all mortal wounds – to calm the mind,
mend the flesh, and bring peace
to the sorrowed soul.*

ODE TO SABNOCK

I speak now to a Marquise of Hell – Sabnock!

I, _____, am a worshipful apostle
of Satan's dominion – hear these
unrepentant words, and heal me from all
that poisons my flesh – sickness,
wickedness, and curses
hissed by pious
tongues!

SINEUS ETUM HETHES

Hear this prayer of mending, Duke Valefor.

In Satan's name, I beckon you – bless this apostle
of Hell, and offer me the breath of devils – I,
_____, seek the eternality of
your throne – hear me, and
bestow upon me your
gift of undying
wellness!

Sineus etum hethes, Valefor.
Ave, Satanas.

A FEARLESS FIRE

O' Gusion – I call upon you now, Duke of Hell!

Hear this infernal prayer, and bless me
with your nature of stillness and
brazen calm – inspirit me with your fearless
fires, and shepherd me to
your gardens of
serenity.

ODE TO PESTILENCE

In search of sanctuary, I call to you – Focalor!

*May I not fall victim to the grim and ghoulish
reaping of Pestilence – he who drowns
the Earth in sallow tides of malady, sat high
atop his pallid horse – the poisoner
of the soul of humanity.*

MIRE OF FEAR

Knight of Hell, bring solace to my path – Furcas!

I, _____, am lost within the nighted gloom
of my mind – howling, groaning – a black
tempest devours me – I am not free
within myself – o' Furcas,
release me from this mire of fear,
and shepherd me to clarity
once again.

HYMNS AND PRAYERS
THAT MAY LEAD TO
DISCOVERY & REVELATIONS

Herein, you will find prayers that pierce through the darkness of life, offering revelations – the discovery of all truths concealed and barred from sight – those things that lurk and prowl where light does not shine.

These revelations – this discovery of all hidden truths and secrecies – it may pertain to the deceit of others, your own ignorance of what lies ahead, or the intent of others – malice masked as goodwill and kindness.

VASSAGO'S VEIL

I speak now to a Prince of Hell – Vassago!

I, _____, seek your cindered sight – lay your veil over my scrying eyes, so that I may witness revelations of the divine – the sins of Heaven, the glory of Hell – all truths that transpire beyond where mortals dwell!

ATULLA PREMOSO

Atulla premoso, Prince Gaap – hear these words!

*Of the past – of a time when all was shrouded
in the shadows of my blindness – reveal
to me what I had not seen, in all
matters pertaining to*

_____.

THE ROAD BEHIND

Hear this prayer, Prince Seere – and guide me!

I have been deceived – led astray and betrayed
in matters of _____ – illuminate
the road behind us, and lead me to where the
treasure of truth lies entombed – buried
beneath the weeping pall
of nightfall.

O' ANDROMALIUS

Heed this infernal prayer, Count Andromalius!

O' Andromalius – I, _____, am
a fervent apostle of our kingdom of Hell, and
I have been transgressed against – reveal
to me the actions of _____,
made in silence behind
my back.

VURTUM SECRIMO

Malphas – spirit of erudition – I call to you now!

*May you bless this apostle of Hell, and offer me
your perception – vurtum secrimo – brilliant
devil, unearth before me the secrets
that lie restless and forgotten – entombed
within the cavernous shadows
of my Left-Hand Path.*

THE ROAD AHEAD

In search of discovery, I call upon you – Valac!

I know not what lies ahead – serpents, gold,

or mysteries prepared to unfold – I,

_____, seek your scrying eyes – may you

look upon my nighted path, and reveal

to me all that awaits beyond

the shadow's edge.

ODE TO AAMON

I speak now to a Marquis of Hell – Aamon!

*Hear this diabolical prayer, and reveal to me
the sulfuric path to power – the brimstone
road that burns in Satan's name, and leads every
apostle to the fruits of our glorious
kingdom of eternal flame!*

Ave, Satanas.

QUISIMO MOLDES

Hear this illuminating prayer, Marquis Phenex!

O' brilliant devil, I stand before you with queries that haunt my mind – heed these words of mine, and make me wise to every unseen truth regarding _____ – deliver unto me the answers that I seek, whether by dream, revelation, or earthly manifestation.

Quisimo moldes apatixa, Phenex!

TORCH OF CIMERIES

Cimeries – devil of shadow – I call to you now!

Hold high your embered torch over my nighted
path, for I have lost sight of _____
amidst the darkness that enshrouds
this brimstone road – help me
reclaim what I have
abandoned!

EXPELLA OCCULO

Barbatos – guide my revelations, Duke of Hell!

My sight has been occluded – I cannot see clearly the path ahead, for it has been devoured beneath the raven fog of magic – expella occulo, Barbatos – cleanse this obfuscation, and allow me to look upon what has been concealed.

NIGHT OF VUAL

I call to you, Vual – unveiler of knowledge!

*As I beckon your sanctuary throne, a chill
enshrouds my bestial heart – it howls in tongues
like winter's tempest, and whispers to me
of brilliance – found within the
darkling depths of your
eternal night.*

WITHIN HER DEPTHS

By silent nightfall, I hail you – Duke Gremory!

This darkness – she holds the knowledge that I desire – hear this wicked prayer, and lift high her starry shroud – reveal to me what secrets have been buried within her dawnless depths!

IN DARKLING FAITH

Flauros, Duchess of Hell – guide this apostle!

*In darkling faith and Satan's name, I walk upon
the Left-Hand Path – make me wise
to all that lies ahead upon this wicked road, and
to all that I may bear witness – danger,
wealth, or the pleasures of our
kingdom of Hell.*

Ave, Satanas.

O' PAIMON

King of Hell, offer me your insight – Paimon!

I, _____ know not what whispers within the heart of _____ – o' Paimon, reveal to me whether they are a harbinger of devilry or goodwill – bring to light their darkest intentions, and what secrets they foster beneath their silence.

PRETAMA REVELLES

Pretama revelles – hear me, King Balam!

All-seeing spirit – devil of revelations, look upon this worshipper of Hell, and reveal to me all that I have not seen – may I become wise to _____, and the things that I have not noticed upon my Left-Hand Path.

THE EYES OF VINE

Hear this covetous prayer, Vine – King of Hell!

O' Vine – fix your burning eyes upon my path,
and show me what I have not seen – lead
me to the fruits of knowledge, and
the revelations that I seek – I,
_____, desire the
wisdom that only
you may set
free.

ADVERSARY OR ALLY

I call to you, Purson – illustrious King of Hell!

I, _____, must know the motives and intent

of _____ – reveal to me what murmurs

in their mortal mind – shall I condemn

them as an adversary, or offer

hearth, as my ally?

HYMNS AND PRAYERS
THAT MAY OFFER
KNOWLEDGE & ILLUMINATION

Herein, you will find prayers that seek the knowledge and illumination of Satan's devils – if the apostle has accepted his burning mark, they may feast beside the spirits of Hell on the blasphemous fruits of brilliance.

These devils shall inspire all corners of the disciple's infernal Left-Hand Path – they may empower rituals, lead one to sagacity, and offer the forbidden wisdom that spills forth from the thrones of Satan's kingdom.

ODE TO IPOS

I speak now to Ipos – great illuminator of Hell!

O' Ipos – ember-kissed prince, I hail your blazing
crown – heed these wicked words, and bless
me with your knowledge – bestow
upon this disciple of Satan
the unholy acumen
of devils.

AMPLIFASSO

Amplifasso occulassa – I call to you, Stolas!

May you hear this apostle of Hell, and inspirit my
Left-Hand Path – breathe your brilliant
fires into my every step, verse, and
sulfuric spellwork – guide me
to infernal orchards
of power!

OF SAGES & DEVILS

Hear me, Haagenti – demoness of enlightenment!

*I, _____, hail your moon-kissed throne
in search of knowledge – may you look upon my
infernal scar, and know me as an apostle
of Hell – fit to inherit the wisdom
of sages and devils!*

THE PALL OF MALPHAS

Malphas – lightless spirit – I call to you now!

Drape your starry pall over my Left-Hand Path,
and bestow upon me the benedictions
of your crown – bless my every word and ritual,
and guide me to the throes of occult
mastery – Malphas, devil
of dawnless night!

ILLYRIA MALLIOS

Illyria mallios – inspirit me, President Caim!

I, _____, seek the blasphemous blessings
of your throne – may the moonlight drip
from your porcelain crown, and
rain wisdom down upon my
Left-Hand Path!

MY BURNING WORD

By witching nightfall, I hail you – President Ose!

With my every burning word, may I witness

the illustrious power of Hell – bless my

Left-Hand Path, and empower

every wicked ritual with

your unhallowed

grace!

ODE TO MARBAS

Make me wise, Marbas – grand architect of Hell!

I, _____, seek the knowledge that seeps
from your cathedraled throne – look
upon my infernal soul, and know me as a sworn
disciple of our kingdom of Hell – bless
me with the ancient wisdom that to humankind
is condemned and forbidden.

HYMNESSIAS

Hymnessias patrimoso – bless me, Leraje!

O' Leraje – demoness of witching grace, I call upon your crown – gaze upon this apostle of Hell, and enchant my Left-Hand Path – breathe your brilliance into my every word and ritual.

ON HERMETIC WINDS

Heed this nighted prayer, Marquis Abraxas!

On Hermetic winds of unhallowed grace, I hear

your witching whispers – disclosures

of power and ancient wisdom,

forbidden to the likes

of humans!

ARTEMOS IMPRESSA

I speak now to a Marquise of Hell – Sabnock!

I, _____, seek the blasphemous brilliance of our kingdom of Hell – of its cinder-kissed devils, and the magic they so artfully wield – in Satan's burning name and honor.

Artemos impressa molgenasso, Sabnock.
Ave, Satanas!

ODE TO APOSTLES

In search of brilliance, I call upon you – Orias!

*Orias – sage of our kingdom of Hell – gaze
upon this apostle's mark, and know that my heart
burns true – in Satan's name, I beckon
you – empower my path with your
diabolical grace, and guide
me to your orchards
of knowledge.*

Ave, Satanas.

DIABOSA ETHES SACRUM

Diabosa ethes sacrum – bless me, Valefor!

I, _____, hail your throne, brilliant galvanizer of Satan's kingdom – may you hear this infernal prayer, and bless this apostle of Hell – gift me with your mastery over all things diabolical and supernatural.

THE LIGHT OF BARBATOS

In search of erudition, I call to you – Barbatos!

Barbatos, light afire my Left-Hand Path – hold
high your cindered torch, and illuminate
the sulfur-paved road towards
brilliance – guide me to the unhallowed
fruits of knowledge, ripened
Satan's name!

Ave, Satanas.

O' ASTAROTH

Hear this errant prayer, Astaroth – Duke of Hell!

*O' Astaroth, bearer of Delphian grace – I,
_____, stand before you an apostle of Hell,
gowned in the glory of Satan's infernal
godhood – may you look upon my ever-burning
scar, and judge me worthy to wield
the brilliance of devils!*

ODE TO PUCEL

Duke of Hell – Pucel, heed this wicked prayer!

*Devil of forbidden knowledge, I beckon
your nighted throne – may you gaze upon this
apostle's heart, and know me as one
of your own – a disciple of Satan, worthy of
the brilliance of our glorious
kingdom of Hell!*

VIVISSIO DAEMAS

Vivissio daemas patiricca – hear me, Vapula!

Of the howling fires, burning without end amidst
our kingdom of Hell – of the shadows
that groan, and the night that never sleeps – of
devils, and all their wicked ways – may
I become wise – I wish to know
all transpires within
the darkness.

THE HORNED APOSTLE

Illustrious spirit, I beckon you – King Balam!

I, _____, am a horned apostle of Satan's congregation, and with a heart of fire, I call upon you now – hear me, and bless me with your brilliance – inspire every wicked ritual I hiss upon my Left-Hand Path.

HYMNS AND PRAYERS
THAT PERTAIN TO
THE BLACK ARTS

Herein, you shall find prayers that pertain to various avenues of the black arts – those paths forbidden to humans, but which may be explored by the disciple that bears the scar of Satan and our kingdom of Hell.

If one is loyal to Satan's godship, these Goetia devils may offer their forbidden knowledge – secrets of the void, the skills of necromancers, and other studies of the occult that have been condemned by humankind.

FROM HEAVEN'S HULL

Prince of Hell, bless my darkling path – Stolas!

Of the stars – those shimmering jewels hung
from Heaven's hull – o' what secrets
they must bear behind ashen
light and nighted air – Stolas, hear
this unholy prayer, and make me wise
to the knowledge sealed within the stars above!

HERMETAS INGLOMIO

Hermetas inglomio – I hail your throne, Marax!

O' Marax – bear witness to this apostle
of Hell, and bless me with your benedictions
of Hermetic brilliance – in witching
whispers to my soul, may you
offer me the wisdom
that I seek.

THE VOID – SHE WHISPERS

By silent starlight, I call to you – President Amy!

The void – she whispers to me in melodies
that soothe my haunted heart – I cannot deny her
darkling grace, nor the beauty of her ebon
deeps – o' Amy, may you reveal to me
your artful ways of wielding
the shadows of her
eternality.

IN WINTER'S NAME

I call to you, Valac – celestial shepherd of Hell!

In winter's chilblained name – as the heavens shimmer, and moonlight drips upon my hellbound path – I, _____, seek your mastery over the star-crested heavens that light my way!

AN EMBERLESS PATH

Hear this prayer, Gamigin – Marquise of Hell!

O' blasphemous devil, heed these words – I,
_____, seek your brilliance in my forbidden
studies of necromancy – the art of the dead,
forgotten flesh, and the souls that have
been abandoned to the hunger of time – Gamigin,
may this apostle of Hell see clearly
upon this emberless path
of death magic!

COSMECCIA

Cosmeccia amogellos, Leraje – hear these words!

Illustrious devil – spirit of cosmic brilliance, gaze
upon this worshipper of Hell, and offer me
your mastery over the heavens – the
groaning abyss, whose starry
depths hold the secrets
of life, death, and
magic.

OF EARTH & ETHER

Abraxas – moonlit devil – I stand before you!

I, _____, call upon you seeking Hermetic brilliance – may I be judged worthy to wield your wisdom of earth and ether – look upon me, and bless me with your knowledge of all that offers life to this strange mortal plane.

ODE TO ORIAS

I speak now to a Marquis of Hell – Orias!

O' Orias, artisan of the abyss – I, _____,

stand before you seeking mastery

over all that lurks within her depths – look upon

my wicked heart, and recognize me

as a disciple of Satan – worthy and fit to wield

your knowledge of the void.

LUNASERE APPIRUM

By ashen starlight, I call to you – Andrealphus!

O' celestial spirit – devil of the immortal abyss,
may you bless me with your mastery over
her darkness – the divine void, and
the strange magic that bubbles
forth from her howling,
Stygian depths.

Lunasere appirum – bless me, Andrealphus!

THE LIGHTLESS CRAFT

I call to you, Eligos – gallant champion of Hell!

*Hear me, and bless this disciple of Satan with
your vulgar knowledge – look upon my
infernal mark, and judge me worthy to receive
your sagacity – make wise this occultist
to the wicked, lightless craft
of necromancy.*

IN SOOT & SHADOW

Murmur, Duke of Hell – enlighten this apostle!

In soot and shadow, I welcome you upon
my Left-Hand Path – Murmur, may you bless me
with your wicked acumen, and guide me to
the blackened fruits of knowledge – I,
_____, seek your mastery
in my unhallowed studies
of necromancy.

HAUTEM ETUUS DI'ABO

Hear this blasphemous prayer, Duke Bune!

*In Satan's name, I call upon you – bless
this acolyte of Hell, and offer me your forbidden
brilliance – I, _____, wish to become
masterful in my studies of life, death,
and the magic that bubbles
between the two.*

*Hautem etuus di'abo.
Ave, Satanas.*

ODE TO ALLOCES

Alloces – devil of darkness – heed this prayer!

May you swing your pallid stars over my nighted
path, and illuminate the brimstone road
ahead – guide me through the fog and shadows,
and lead me to brilliance – make wise
this apostle of Hell, and offer
me your knowledge
of the abyss.

FROM THE FIRES

May you empower my Left-Hand Path – Furcas!

O' Furcas – hear me, and inspirit me with your
kindling grace – may I, _____, tear
brilliance and visions from the fires
of our kingdom of Hell – o'
cindered devil, bless
this apostle of
Satan!

OF BLOOD & DARKNESS

King of Hell – Zagan, hear this infernal prayer!

*Zagan, devil of blood and darkness – I,
_____, stand before you a beast of Hell,
gowned in the flames of Satan's errant
godhood – may you look upon my ever-burning
scar, and judge me worthy to embrace
the vampiric brilliance of
your crown!*

HYMNS AND PRAYERS
THAT MAY OFFER
METAPHYSICALITY

Herein, you will find prayers that may offer unholy gifts to apostles of Satan – metaphysical abilities that defy the natural boundaries of mortals, offered by the generosity of devils – our cindered saints of hellfire.

The Goetia devils shall bestow upon the worthy their supernatural aptitudes – clairvoyance, premonitory sight, and transmutative knowledge – the abilities of demons, forbidden by God to the likes of humankind.

SHEPHERD OF SOULS

Prince of Hell, offer me your blessings – Ipos!

O' Ipos, shepherd of souls – I, _____, seek

your awareness – your unearthly ability to

sense the supernatural, and to guide

the paths of the departed – to

ritual, celebration, or

the ebon gates of our kingdom

of Hell!

ADELPHIA VISUCCI

Adelphia visucci, Orobas – hear these words!

*Of the path that lies ahead, shrouded
beneath the lightless fog of mystery – may you
reveal to me what gloams in wait,
through the visions, dreams, and auguries
that spill forth from your
moonlit throne.*

OF SOULS DEPARTED

I speak now to Bifrons – mystic Count of Hell!

*Hear this lightless rite, and bless me
with your clairvoyant sight – may I, _____,
become wise to the presence of spirits, and may
I call upon them as I desire – by the grim
tongues of those souls departed.*

THE SIGHT OF CAIM

President of Hell, lend me your sight – Caim!

I cannot see what gloams within the darkness
that surrounds me – the hissing viper,
the hungering beast – or, for better, the fruits
of Satan's kingdom – o' Caim, hear
me, and bless me with your clairvoyant vision!

INNUX ETUUS XUNNI

Innux etuus xunni – bless me, President Marbas!

Devil of ancient knowledge – I, _____,

seek your brilliance in the ancient ways

of transmutation – lead unto gold,

and sorrow unto strength – I

must become an artisan

of metamorphic

magic!

DAMNED & DEPARTED

Gamigin – empower my path, Marquise of Hell!

O' Gamigin, orchestrator of mortal souls – I,

_____, call upon you in search

of clairvoyance – may you make

me wise to the workings

of the damned and

departed!

PRETACCIO MEDUMASI

Pretaccio medumasi – I call to you, Abraxas!

O' Abraxas – hear this disciple of Hell,
and bless me with your oracular sight – whether
by dream or witching augury – in the stars
or by lamplight's ember – may I
bear witness to all things
yet to transpire!

THE CHILL OF MURMUR

By midnight's chill, I call to you – Duke Murmur!

With my every blasphemous word, may I witness
the workings of the damned – those spirits
that toil upon this pallid mortal coil,
bearing fruits of brilliance
from beyond their
icy graves!

ODE TO BERITH

Berith – spirit of augury – I call upon you now!

Look fondly upon this apostle of Satan, and
bless me with your oracular sight – I,
_____, desire visions of
all things to come – o'
Berith, devil of
divination!

TO SEE – TO DREAM

Hear me, Astaroth – devil of revelation!

I, _____, wish to see – to dream in visions of witching augury – o' Astaroth, lend me your divining sight – make me wise to all that awaits me upon waking, and to all that this mortal life has fated me.

OF GLORY & GRANDEUR

Heed this wicked prayer, King Bael!

*Bael, devil of glory and grandeur – I,
_____, stand before you an apostle of Hell,
prepared for your benedictions – may you
bestow upon me your Delphian
gaze, and the augural
visions of your
throne!*

HYMNS AND PRAYERS
THAT MAY BRING
WEALTH, RICHES & SUCCESS

Herein, you will find prayers that entreat entry to the mountainous, gilded coffers of Hell – where fortunes are offered to all that bear the burning scar of Satan, and no apostle must ignore their desire for grandeur.

If the disciple should desire wealth, riches, or earthly furtherment, these prayers shall come in use – for the Goetia devils are generous, and they shall offer every mortal splendor to those judged worshipful of Satan.

HIS GILDED FIRES

Count of Hell – Raum, hear this covetous prayer!

Devil of pilfered fortunes, I invoke
your lightless throne – may you gaze upon this
disciple's mark, and know me as one
of your own – bless me with your gilded fires,
and guide me to the boundless
riches of our kingdom
of Hell!

ODE TO ANDROMALIUS

By nighted hellfire, I hail you – Andromalius!

Hear me, illustrious devil, and bless this apostle

of Hell with your coffers overspilled – I,

_____, call upon you now in

search of boundless riches

in the infernal name

of Satan!

Ave, Satanas.

THE PATH TO WEALTH

I speak now to a President of Hell – Amy!

I, _____, wish to walk your embered
path to wealth, riches, and opulence – reveal to
me the brimstone road paved with
gold and the luxurious fires
of our kingdom
of Hell!

OCEANS OF GOLD

In search of fortune, I call upon you – Foras!

Foras – miser of our kingdom of Hell – I,

_____, call upon your avaricious crown in

search of riches, and the boundless wealth

of devils – accept this apostle before

your coffers, and flood my

path with oceans

of gold!

COFFICCI ALORIDA

Cofficci alorida, Marbas – hear this prayer!

*O' Marbas – devil of gilded sight, I call
upon your throne – bless this apostle of Satan,
and illuminate my Left-Hand Path – reveal
to me the cindered road to wealth,
whereupon lies the coffers
of our kingdom
of Hell!*

OF GILDED FLAME

In Satan's shadow, I hail you – Duke Sallos!

*Hear me, Sallos – devil of gilded flame
and grandeur – I, _____, call upon you in
search of boundless wealth – bless this
disciple of Hell, and grant me
entry to your coffers
overflown!*

THE FRUITS OF GUSION

O' lauded spirit, I beckon you – Gusion!

I, _____, am a horned apostle of Satan's kingdom, and I call upon you now in his blackened name – hear this prayer, and bless me with the fruits earthly betterment – may success and opportunity flood my Left-Hand Path!

Ave, Satanas.

INSPIRIA VI'ELLA

Inspiria vi'ella – hear me, Duke Eligos!

*I, _____, hail your crown in search
of earthly success, and the inextinguishable glory
of our kingdom of Hell – bless me, and
seed your fruits of furtherance
upon my ember-paved
Left-Hand Path!*

MY WEALTH RETURNED

Duke of Hell – Gremory, hear these words!

O' Gremory, revealer of all things lost, damned,
and abandoned – return to me the mortal
fruits that I have let spoil – wealth,
and the riches squandered by
the idle hands of this
apostle of Hell.

ODE TO ASMODEUS

I speak now to a King of Hell – Asmodeus!

Hear this avaricious prayer, and bestow upon me
the fruits of your cindered throne – look
upon my infernal mark, and flood my hellbound
path with riches, wealth, and grandeur
without end – in Satan's name,
may it be so!

Ave, Satanas.

HYMNS AND PRAYERS
THAT MAY INSPIRE
LOVE, SEX & HEDONISM

Herein, you will find prayers that shepherd one to the doorstep of hedonistic splendor – where apostles and demons are free to celebrate their nature – as beasts of Satan, unbound to guilt for their carnal appetites.

These spirits shall aid the apostle in their pursuit of all bestial satiations – should one desire love, sex, or the embrace of their hedonistic nature, they shall find sanctuary before the moaning thrones of these devils.

VASSAGO'S HEARTH

Hear this prayer, Vassago – Prince of Hell!

Vassago, devil of kindling – light afire
my Left-Hand Path, and attract to me all matter
of love, lust, and passion – may this apostle
enjoy hearth unbridled, and the
fervency that denotes
your throne.

HEDONOS APPETIVA

Hedonos appetiva, Sitri – hear these words!

I, _____, seek the guiltless pleasures of our kingdom of Hell – its sensual fruits, and all luxuries of the flesh – may you delight in these words, and bestow upon me the carnal satiations of your crown!

HEARTH & HELLFIRE

Prince of Hell, bless my wicked path – Gaap!

Amorous spirit – devil of burning hearth and
hellfire, gaze upon this apostle of Satan,
and bless my bestial heart – bestow upon me
the fires of love, and a muse to call
my own – Prince Gaap,
hear this ardent
prayer!

CUPIDASO PROVOCCI

Cupidaso provocci – hear me, Countess Furfur.

Hear me, and bless this disciple of Satan with

unquenchable love – set afire the heart of

_____, in my name – may

our souls smolder as one,

in Hell's eternal

flames.

ODE TO RAUM

Count of Hell – Raum, hear this prayer!

*O' Raum, bless this apostle of Hell – look
upon the heart of _____, and
kindle within its darkling atria the fires
of desire – may their spirit burn
for me eternally.*

HARMONISSO

Aamon – devil of desire – I call to you now!

*Hear me, Aamon, and reignite
the infernal fires that bind _____ and
I – in Satan's name, may harmony
once again thrive between
our wild souls!*

*Harmonisso apitixia – bless me, Aamon!
Ave, Satanas!*

ATTELLIS PI'RUUA

Attellis pi'ruua, Leraje – hear these words!

Marquise of Hell, bless this disciple of Satan
with your hypnotic nature
and the allure of your spirit – I, _____,
wish to attract those that I
desire, and those that may offer pleasure
to my Left-Hand Path.

O' FORNEUS

I speak now to Forneus – noble spirit of Hell!

I, _____, desire the love and hearth of another's heart – o' Forneus, bless me, and set upon my path a muse to call my own – one who cherishes me, and shall forever entwine their hellbound soul with mine.

GARDEN OF MARCHOSIAS

Marchosias – bless my path, Marquise of Hell!

I, _____, hail your crown, o' witching temptress of Satan's apostles – hear this prayer, and bestow upon me the pleasures of your throne – that moaning garden, wherefrom blooms all carnal fruits!

HYMN OF SALLOS

Duke of Hell, bless my bestial path – Sallos!

O' Sallos – carnal devil, I call upon you
in search of love – the union of heart and soul,
bound by the fires of Hell – o' Sallos,
spirit of pleasure – shepherd
unto me the affections
of _____.

ONCE – TWICE MINE

By Hell's emberlight, I call to you – Gusion!

I, _____, stand before you an apostle

of Satan's congregation – bless me,

and return to me the muse that I have lost – may

the heart of _____ thunder my

name once more – and, once

again, may our mortal

souls entwine.

SUCCUBI OF ZEPAR

Hear this hedonistic prayer, Duke Zepar!

*I, _____, call upon you now in search
of a succubi familiar – a demoness of Hell, eager
to pleasure and please this apostle
of Satan's kingdom – may she covet me, and love
me eternally – may I feel her lustful
touch as I live and breathe,
until I descend to
Perdition.*

CARNALLA ETUUS HEDOMOS

Carnalla etuus hedomos – hear me, Vual!

I, _____, wish to feast upon the fruits of pleasure – to taste the ambrosial bounties of our Lord Satan, and rejoice in my hedonistic nature – o' Vual, may we dine together upon the moaning spirit of carnality!

MALLAMIA SUCCUMOS

Mallamia succumos – bless me, Duke Gremory!

I, _____, seek the pleasurous embrace
of a succubus familiar – may you look
upon this apostle of Hell, and
offer me the company
of a lecherous demoness – bound
by your throne, and sworn
to this loyal disciple
of Satan!

ODE TO ZAGAN

Heed this blasphemous hymn, King Zagan!

In Satan's name, I call upon you – aid
this acolyte of Hell, and heal the severed sinews
that once bound me to _____ – I,
_____ desire the rekindling
of your throne – hear me,
and offer me your
salvation!

Ave, Satanas.

O' BELETH

Beleth – bring passion to my path, King of Hell!

O' Beleth, devil of love, lust, and lechery – I,

_____, call upon you now seeking

the heart of _____ – may it

thunder in my name, and

forever burn with

adoration!

HYMNS AND PRAYERS
THAT CALL FOR
TRUTH & VENGEANCE

Herein, you will find prayers that seek order, justice, truth, and vengeance – the pursuit of retribution and penance – if any apostle of Satan would fall victim to wickedness, they shall be avenged a thousandfold.

May no beast of Hell suffer wrongdoing at the hands of the pious – may no intruder prevail over a horned disciple of Satan – these devils of the Goetia shall aid in the punishment of all sinners – an eye for an eye.

THE FURY OF FURFUR

Countess of Hell, aid this disciple – Furfur!

In Satan's name, avenge this worshipful apostle of Hell – I, _____, have fallen prey to the cruelty of _____ – cull this lamb from my Left-Hand Path, and thrash upon them the fury of your tempestuous throne!

Ave, Satanas.

IN BLOOD AND MOONFALL

In search of reprisal, I call to you – Halphas!

Halphas – vicious devil, armored in the blood and moonfall of damnation – stand before me, and heap your vehemence upon _____ – a transgressor upon this disciple's nighted path!

DEBALMA AXEGASO

Andromalius – avenge me, great Count of Hell!

I, _____, seek the cleansing fires
of your cinder-sworn throne – debalma axegaso,
Andromalius – purge from my path the
transgressor that stands before us – may you cast
_____ unto sorrow's throes, for
they have sinned against this
apostle of Satan!

THE COURT OF MINOS

I speak now to a President of Hell – Marax!

Hear this unhallowed prayer, and cast the soul

of _____ before the insidious court

of Minos – judge of the damned,

and deliverer of justice in

the name of Satan!

Ave, Satanas.

INSALLOS MEDUMIA

Insallos medumia, Malphas – hear my words!

I, _____, wish to defile the mind of my adversary – may _____ wither and fall prey to the decay of sanity – torment their spirit, and envenom their every thought with madness!

WINTER'S BLIGHT

Beneath midnight's pall, I call to you – Ose!

As winter blights the loam of Earth,
may you blight the soul of _____ – wrap
your chilblained hands around their
heart, and flood its atria with
the howling sorrow of
your throne!

A SOUL CONDEMNED

May you punish my adversary, Marquis Ronove!

*Ruthless spirit – shepherd of the forsaken, guide
the bastard soul of _____ to the gates
of Hell – cast them before Minos, and
he shall surely condemn them
to the circle that reflects
their wicked sins!*

GRIEVIASSO

Hear this blasphemous prayer, Marquis Shax!

*In Satan's name, I call upon you – abet
this acolyte of Hell, and smite the trespasser that
has erred against me – may _____
inherit your callous wrath, and
suffer penance for their
transgressions!*

Grieviasso vautemo matirrix, Shax!
Ave, Satanas.

EXECUMA TERRIDOS

Execuma terridos – avenge me, Marquis Andras!

I call upon your wicked throne in search of retribution – _____ has sworn conflict against this apostle of Satan, and I must witness their penance – cast their quivering soul unto the blackest pitch and gloom of our kingdom of Hell!

ODE TO ELIGOS

Hear me, Eligos – devil of righteous hellfire!

I, _____, stand now before the scales
of earthly judgment – to be penanced, and to face
chastisements from the lambs – o' Eligos,
hear me, and protect me in the trials
that lie ahead – may I find good
fortune in the outcome
of _____.

THE FIRES OF FLAUROS

I call to you, Flauros – grim Duchess of Hell!

O' Flauros, demoness of vehement grace – hear
me, and bathe my adversary within
the fires of your throne – scorch the bastard soul
of _____, and leave upon it your
weeping stigmata – given to those
that sin against Satan's
loyal apostles!

VINE'S TITHE

Vine – formidable spirit – I call to you now!

Hear this prayer, and possess the wretched soul of _____ – tear the light from our transgressor, and plunge them into the blackest malebolge of our kingdom of Hell – in Satan's name, may they only know darkness for all their remaining days.

HYMNS AND PRAYERS
THAT SPEAK OF
GENERAL WICKEDNESS

Herein, you shall find prayers that call upon the raw and unrepentant rage of our kingdom of Hell – these unholy hymns call for wickedness and sorrow, aimed against the transgressors of Satan's loyal disciples.

If the apostle has been sinned against by another, the prayers within this chapter shall offer a path to swift retribution – destruction, misery, plague, and further words of rancor may be found in the hymns ahead.

OF HOWLING TEMPESTS

I speak now to Furfur – Countess of Hell!

*Devil of howling tempests, I invoke
your wicked throne – may you look over this
disciple's path, and summon forth
your raging storms – to cleanse and defend
me from all that bears malice,
and those that would
trespass against this apostle
of Satan's godship.*

RAUM'S RUINATION

In nighted grace, I hail you – Count Raum!

O' Raum, fix your ruinating gaze upon
the reputation of _____ – may they become
a leper amongst mortal lambs, and
a pariah to those they love
and cherish.

HYSPIRIA MOLLOM

Hyspiria mollom, Andromalius – hear my words!

I, _____, seek your mastery over
the mortal mind – may I become an artisan of
deception, capable of weaving the will
and whim of those that I judge
fit – Andromalius, bless
me with this most
unholy gift!

THE MIND'S DECAY

President of Hell, aid this loyal acolyte – Ose!

I, _____, hail your crown, o' wicked haunter of mortalkind – hear this heinous prayer, and tear the light of sanity from my transgressor, _____ – may madness smother their every thought, and spread chaos throughout their mind!

SOUL & SINEWS

Heed this wicked prayer, President Marbas!

*O' Marbas, architect of Hell – I desire
the ruination of _____ – may the light of
their soul fall black with soot, and may
the sinews unravel from their brittle bones – o'
Marbas, may you spread discord
within our unrepentant
adversary!*

DAEMOS ETUUS CARRAS

Daemos etuus carras – hear me, Glasya-Labolas!

As I traverse this blasphemous Left-Hand Path,
may I not journey alone – bestow upon
me the guard of your familiar devils, bound
eternally to my diabolical soul – in
Satan's name, may I inherit
this blessing from your
vicious throne!

Ave, Satanas.

THE CRUEL & THE PIOUS

Marquis of Hell – Ronove, heed this prayer!

Devil of unhallowed grace, I beckon
your nighted throne – hear this apostle of Hell,
and bestow upon me your ability to
weaken the willpower of those that sin against
me – the cruel, the pious, and those
that dare trespass upon my
Left-Hand Path.

LOVE, UNDONE

Leraje – cindered demoness – I stand before you!

I call to you with malice in my words – hear me,
and putrefy the dearest bonds enjoyed by
my adversary, _____ – may
Cupid forsake their bastard heart, and separate
them from their beloved – alone,
and never to feel again the warmth
of their weeping
arms.

HAUTELLAS AMORTEMA

Heed this nighted hymn, Marquis Andrealphus!

May your whispers carry on the winds
of my Left-Hand Path – hissing in wicked tongues
that incite madness within the minds
of trespassers – hautellas amortema – eclipse
the road ahead within the murmuring
shadows of your throne – o'
Andrealphus, sinister
Marquis of Hell!

THE HAUNTING OF AGARES

By Hell's emberlight, I call to you – Agares!

Hear me, grim demoness, and possess
the pallid spirit of _____ – a provocateur,
and an adversary of this devoted apostle
of Satan's congregation – drag
their soul into the blackest depths
of our kingdom
of Hell!

ODE TO AIM

I call to you, Aim – embered Duke of Hell!

I, _____, seek the cataclysms
of your crown – may flame and cinders rain down
from the skies above my unhallowed
Left-Hand Path – annihilate all that awaits me
bearing malice and malcontent – cleanse
the shadowed road ahead for
this worshipful disciple
of our kingdom
of Hell!

O' FOCALOR

Hear this vulgar prayer, Focalor – Duke of Hell!

O' Focalor, deliverer of torment to the unjust,
the wicked, and the pious – hear me,
and slate the soul of _____ for suffering
without reprieve – for they have sinned
against this embered apostle of
Satan's congregation!

OF SPECTERS AND ILLUSIONS

By moonrise, I beckon you – Duchess Vepar!

Our trespasser – _____ – seize their sanity,
and rend their mind of every sallow
strand of light – leave
them to darkness – there, where
specters jeer from the shadow's shroud,
and visions arise of terrible things – aberrations,
and devils dancing – dreadful illusions
that should not be, yet haunt
the edge of periphery!

AN EPOCH OF MADNESS

In Satan's eclipse, I call to you – Duke Pucel!

Hear me, Pucel – I, _____, call to you
in search of delirium – commandeer
the feeble mind of _____, and usher forth
an epoch of fear, chaos, and absolute
madness – may they smother
beneath the ebon tides
of insanity!

MEDUNNAS LI'BELLOS

Medunnas li'bellos – hear me, Dantalion!

May _____'s mind wither and rot within your eclipse, Dantalion – plague this lamb with visions of the damned, and what most fills their heart with dread – may their life become torment, and may sleep offer no escape from your unrelenting terror!

ODE TO CHAOS

Vine, King of Hell – bear witness to this prayer!

*In Satan's name, I seek chaos upon
the path of _____ – this bastard lamb has
transgressed against an apostle of Hell,
and they must lament for their
sins – may the Earth
shatter beneath their feet, and
may the heavens weep flame and embers
upon their aspect – destroy all roads
that may lead them to sanctuary.*

Ave, Satanas.

THE WITHERING OF BAEL

Bael – illustrious devil – I call to you now!

O' Bael, god-king of Hell – hear me,
and putrefy the mind of _____ – may they
wither in lucidity, and sow the seeds
of chaos upon their very path – may their own
hand turn against them, and spread
sorrow like plagues
bubonic!

HYMNS AND PRAYERS
THAT MAY OFFER
CONQUEST, STATUS & PRESTIGE

Herein, you will find prayers that aim to steel nerves, offer advancements in life, and bring profound honor to the disciple's path – that brimstone road of glory, paved with fire, and fated to every form of greatness.

These infernal hymns call upon the thrones of Hell's most prestigious devils – those that radiate authority, honor, and dignification – and they will offer Satan's apostles every opportunity to share in this grandeur.

GIANT OF OLDE

I call to you, Amy – revered President of Hell!

I, _____, seek a seat of earthly power – may my name carry like thunder, and may my tread quake this mortal loam like the dying groans of Goliath – giant of olde!

AUTIGRA DOMINES

Autigra domines – hear me, Marquis Aamon!

Stalwart spirit – devil of infernal grace,
look upon this worshipper of Hell, and bless me
with your nature – may I become bold,
and capable of commanding
those that turn to me
for guidance.

HOLLIMOS ETHES NI'TIRRA

Hollimos ethes ni'tirra – bless me, Cerberus!

*I, _____, wish to receive the power
of your throne – of heads thrice, howling in fury
at the firmament above – o' Cerberus,
bestow upon me a position of
earthly glory, in the name of our
indomitable kingdom
of Hell!*

ODE TO FORNEUS

Marquis of Hell, hear these words – Forneus!

O' Forneus, heed this apostle's prayer – I,
_____, call upon your crown in pursuit of
illustrious acclaim – gown me within
your infernal grace, and gild
my earthly name – may I know only
grandeur for what remains
of my mortal days!

AN EIDOLON OF POWER

In search of supremacy, I beckon you – Orias!

Of the fires – howling, and lashing the shadows
of our nighted kingdom – of this mortal
Earth, plagued by those of frail
constitution – may I tower indomitably – an
eidolon of power, whose presence
commands respect within
every soul that I
encounter!

OF GUSION'S GRACE

Duke Gusion, hear this blasphemous prayer!

Bestow upon this apostle of Satan
the prestige of your throne – that aura of infernal
grandeur that demands the respect
of men and devils – o' Gusion,
may I inherit the grace
of your burning
crown!

LUCIFUGE, THE ARBITER

I speak now to a Duke of Hell – Focalor!

O' Focalor, may you look upon my cindered scar,
and know me as an acolyte of Hell – hear
me, and bless me with the favor
of he that shares the blood of Satan – Lucifuge,
arbiter of our kingdom of perpetual
darkness – may he know me
as a sworn devotee of
Satan's godship!

OF SATAN'S CHOSEN

King of Hell, hear this disciple – Paimon!

Paimon – gild my name in the glorious infernos
of our kingdom of Hell – may I inherit
the prestige of your throne,
and be hailed by apostles and devils
the same – look upon my brand, and know that
my heart burns true – I am worthy,
and I am fit to receive the
honor of Satan's
chosen.

AMONGST DEVILS

I call to you now, Belial – King of Hell!

*O' Belial, may this apostle be welcomed
amongst the devils of Hell – reveal to all infernal
spirits my burning mark, and they shall
accept me as their kin – a loyal
apostle of Satan's reign
and our glorious
kingdom of
sin!*

IMEXIAS ETUUS SATANAS

Imexias etuus Satanas – bless me, King Bael!

In Satan's graces, may I, _____, find myself – may he favor me as a worshipful apostle, and offer entry to our bacchanal kingdom of Hell – that groaning sanctuary for mortal beasts and his blasphemous devils of legend!

HYMNS AND PRAYERS
THAT MAY IMPART
THE NATURE OF DEVILS

Herein, you shall find prayers that bestow the unique traits and talents of devils upon disciples – those that are judged loyal to Satan's reign shall become of his legions – in mind, character, personality, and ability.

If an apostle bears the mark of Hell, they may inherit the attributes of its spirits – cunning, perception, and gifts of artistry – song, verse, and all other aptitudes that pique the interest of humans and demons, alike.

IN MY HONOR

By Hell's cinderlight, I call to you – Ipos!

*I, _____, seek confidence and the poise
of your ivoried throne – may I stand
unabashed in the face of life's intimidations,
for I am an unrepentant
beast of Satan's congregation – I am
resilient, and the strength of Hell
surges throughout my
howling heart!*

CHARICASSO DAEMAS

President of Hell – Foras, hear these words!

May I inherit the nature of Hell's most illustrious devils – make me wise, enigmatic, and indomitable – charicasso daemas, Foras – hear me, and inspirit me with the attributes of Satan's chosen – reshape me, and empower me with your burning spirit!

THE LOAM OF EDEN

In darkling grace, I hail you – President Valac!

O' Valac, illustrious devil of the night – I,
_____, call upon your frostbound throne in
pursuit of the nature of serpents – reshape
me, and inspirit me with cunning,
guile, and wickedness – may I become
like he who first trespassed
upon the holy loam
of Eden!

OF TONGUE & VERSE

I speak now to a Marquis of Hell – Phenex!

*Of floral tongue and poetic verse, may I
become masterful – imbue me with your artistic
fire, so that I may conquer the pen and
parchment – so that I may to bring to life the
songs of the heart, and arouse
the passions of one's
eternal soul.*

ODE TO ANDREALPHUS

I call to you, Andrealphus – Marquis of Hell!

Hear me, and bless this disciple of Satan with
your cunning nature – may I become
one with the shadows, whose darkling tides glide
across the Earth with grace – I wish to be
as guileful as the night, and those
devils that lurk beneath
her covers.

HIS SILVER LYRE

Cimeries – devil of perception – heed this prayer!

O' Cimeries, bless me with your spaded
tongue – that silver lyre of witching charm that
may enchant by word and word alone – I
wish to speak with guile, wit, and
rhetoric – to captivate all
that would hear my
voice.

LANGUILLA ETUUS DAEMAS

Languilla etuus daemas – hear me, Agares!

I, _____, call upon your crown
in search of linguistic brilliance – bless me with
your knowledge of demonic tongues,
so that I may hold council with my kinsmen
amidst the ancient flames of
Satan's kingdom!

TO SPEAK AS SPIRITS

I speak now to a Duke of Hell – Barbatos!

*O' Barbatos – devil of illumination, bless
me with your linguistic brilliance – may I become
wise to all aberrant tongues, and the
ancient dialects of devils – I
wish to speak as spirits do, and converse
with the infernal denizens of our
kingdom of Hell!*

THE EYE OF AIM

Aim – cindered spirit – I beckon your throne!

*Hear me, Aim – devil of vicious flame
and brilliance – I, _____, call upon you in
quest for your perceptive nature – bless this
disciple of Hell, and bestow upon
me your all-seeing eye
and intuition.*

IN VUAL'S EMBRACE

In pursuit of fortitude, I beckon you – Vual!

Devil of blackened grace, I call to your
wintered throne – heed this blasphemous prayer,
and enshroud me within your icy chill – I,
_____, seek the confidence
for which you are known – o' Vual, may I
stand brazen and tall like the ebon
ramparts of our kingdom
of Hell!

THE TRUMPETS OF HELL

Amdusias – empower my path, Duke of Hell!

O' Amdusias, may I rejoice in the sounds
of Hell – the reverie of celebrants, and the dismal
carol of the trumpeters – may I learn to sing
their dreadful songs, and pen an opus
in praise of Satan – fill me with
the music of the damned
and their unholy
acumen!

HYMNS AND PRAYERS
THAT PERTAIN TO
DIVINE BLASPHEMY

Herein, you shall find prayers that pursue knowledge from ethereal worlds and kingdoms, concealed from the ignorant eyes of mortalkind – where gods, devils, and other immortal beings dwell with perpetuity.

As well as wisdom, these Goetia devils may bless the apostles of Satan with unfathomable acts of infernal dignification – immortality, rebirth, and shepherding to the gates of our glorious kingdom of Hell.

DI'AMESSIA OCCULLIOS

Di'amessia occullios, Stolas – hear my words!

Of archives hidden behind pallid clouds
or embered mountains – of the abyss, and worlds
within her darkling deeps – bring to light
the knowledge locked away by keys
divine – what secrets lie
within the libraries
of the gods?

AS HEAVEN SPILLS OVER

Countess of Hell, bring me brilliance – Furfur!

O' wicked demoness, bless this apostle
of Hell with forbidden knowledge – of Heaven,
and God – may the primeval secrets
of that divine plane spill upon
my infernal path like
angelic rain!

SECRIMOS ETHUS DAEMAS

O' Caim – devil of shadow – I hail your crown!

I, _____, seek the coveted knowledge
of devils – the secrets barred behind lock and key
from the infantile eyes of humanity – may
you look upon my infernal mark,
and know me as an apostle
of Hell – fit to inherit
the wisdom that
I desire!

Secrimos ethus daemas – enlighten me, Caim!

OF HEAVEN PILLAGED

Heed this blasphemous prayer, Glasya-Labolas!

*May we peel back the pall of God, and his sallow
kingdom of servants – may we unveil his
wisdom secreted, and all truths
barred by the hands of angels from the eyes
of humankind – o' Glasya-Labolas,
may we feast upon the fruits
of Heaven pillaged!*

BEHIND IVORY GATES

I call to you, Andrealphus – Marquis of Hell!

O' Andrealphus, hear this unhallowed prayer and
bless me with your revelations – bestow
upon this celebrant of Satan your knowledge
of angelic secrets – may I become wise
to all that Heaven hides, and
to all that transpires
behind its ivory
gates.

HER APHOTIC SECRETS

In search of erudition, I beckon you – Valefor!

I, _____, wish to look upon the fruits
of our universe – the aphotic secrets of the void,
sequestered away from the scrying eyes
of humankind – o' Valefor, bless
my Left-Hand Path with the
hidden knowledge
of the abyss!

ODE TO BATHIN

Duchess of Hell, bless this disciple – Bathin!

By the emberlight of Hell, may you reveal to me
the secrets that you keep – of angelic
thrones and truths divine – o' Bathin, may I
taste the nectar of these pilfered
fruits – the bounties of
Eden's ruin.

DAEMOSO ETUUS OMNISSIA

Daemoso etuus omnissia – hear me, Pucel!

*O' Pucel – devil of unhallowed grace, I call
upon your crown – gaze upon this apostle's mark,
and shepherd me to the gates of Hell – to
our kingdom of fire, where I shall
inherit a throne of power – beside you,
and my kinsmen – where we shall
reign and revel alongside
our Lord Satan!*

WHERE SATAN REIGNS

I speak now to Alloces – brilliant Duke of Hell!

If I should take my final breath, and the life escapes my glinted eyes, may Death pass over my bedside – for my soul is inextinguishable, and I am fated to the kingdom of Hell – there, I shall be reborn – where Satan reigns and my kinsmen revel amidst darkness and flames sempiternal!

VAPULA'S HEARTH

Duchess of Hell, bless my errant path – Vapula!

Wintered spirit – demoness of hearth and ancient
brilliance, I call upon you now – bless
this apostle of Satan with the
knowledge of your
icebound crown – bestow upon me
the forbidden wisdom
of devils!

HEIMESIO ETUUS PATRIXIA

Heimesio etuus patrixia – bless me, King Zagan!

In Satan's cindered name – as the Heavens
roll and heave over this apostle's blackened path,
may wisdom rain down and flood the road
ahead – with knowledge divine, and
angelic secrets – of the truth
that lies hidden in the
pallid kingdom
of God!

CLOSING HONORS

I extend my gratitude to my fellow clergymen, and those that have abetted this manuscript's creation.

The members and associates of this ministry have offered support in myriad ways – *all* of which have abetted my direction as our overseeing minister.

Rev. Dante – I thank you for your editing over our manuscripts, and your guidance in crucial times.

Rev. Malachi – I thank you for the reach that your mentors have provided us, in occult communities.

Bishop – I thank you for the endless resources and opportunities that you have offered this ministry.

OTHER PUBLICATIONS

The Infernal Gospel

The Goetia Hymns

The Satanic Philosopher

Ars Diabolica

Ars Animarum

Ars Aeterna

Ars Sanguinea

Ars Exitialis

The Abyssal Bible – Coming Soon

The Hierophant of Hell – Coming Soon

You may find us on Facebook, as well as on Etsy, where we offer our world-renowned demonological grimoires, occult antiques, and *numerous* Left-Hand Path oddities.

For business inquiries, please use the messaging feature on Etsy and contact us directly – if your inquiries regard wholesale purchase of our paperback books, we cannot directly assist you – it **is** something that we offer, but it must be done via Amazon KDP's business services, and we cannot facilitate the process in any meaningful way.

Facebook: @OfficialRevCain

Etsy: TheInfernalCircle

www.theinfernalcircle.com

www.ingramcontent.com/pod-product-compliance
Ingram Content Group UK Ltd.
Pitfield, Milton Keynes, MK11 3LW, UK
UKHW021303230225
4720UKWH00020B/179